MOONSONG LULLABY

MOONSONG LULLABY

by Jamake Highwater
photographs by Marcia Keegan

Lothrop, Lee & Shepard Books/New York

Library of Congress Cataloging in Publication Data
Highwater, Jamake./Moonsong Lullaby.
Summary: As the moon moves across the sky, it observes the activities of an Indian camp and of the natural
phenomena surrounding it.   [1. Indians of North America—Fiction.   2. Night—Fiction]   I. Keegan, Marcia.
II. Title. PZ7.H5443Mo   [E]   81-1909
ISBN 0-688-00427-X   AACR2   ISBN 0-688-00428-8 (lib. bdg.)

To Dorothy,
who gave my words freedom

Listen carefully, child.
The Moon moves into the evening sky,
her soft light streaming through the treetops.
She is singing, singing to the People of the campfire.

Tonight there are many good campfires.
Our men are home from the hunt
with the mighty deer who died for us today.
And from the ferny paths of the forest
we have speckled eggs and wild berries and pine nuts.

The Moon sings
across the mountains
as our mothers cook
over our many fires.
We give thanks
to the deer for meat,
to the birds for eggs,
to the earth
for berries and nuts.

The night is filled
with animal people who sleep
and those who do not sleep.
Rabbit and Fox dream in their burrows,
while from the tall pine
Owl hoots softly.
Opossum makes her little snorting sounds.
High in the sky a lone hawk circles,
tirelessly praising the moonlight.

Mushrooms spring up in the cool damp of the darkness,
and lilies unfold pale blooms.
Roots nuzzle the good earth, burrowing into the depths
where silent waters flow.

Our holy people sit in the tall grass and watch
two hundred times two hundred bats
spin and flutter toward the Moon.
Soon our Wise Ones will step through the sweetgrass,
seeking the healing herbs that hide there.

As the Moon climbs high
grandmothers talk of the old days
and of the ways they knew when they were young.
Grandfathers tell of wondrous things told to them
by their fathers and their fathers' fathers.
Their stories speak to us across the years,
of things we must know
if the Moon is to smile on us
as she sings her song.

The night is shelter
for those who weep.
The darkness is filled
with the loneliness of those
whose loved ones have gone away.
The Moon caresses their brown faces,
turning tears into glimmering beadwork—
adornment to ease the hour of sorrow.

A pinecone falls in the perfect stillness.
Lovers sigh and cling close together
as the night nears its deepest hour.

Above the mountains mist-dancers rise
in luminous clouds, leaping gracefully,
ever so slowly into the moonlit sky.

The night promises good tomorrows.
The Moon is singing to her husband,
who sleeps in the dark mountains.
He will rise in the morning,
strong and bright, but for now
the mighty golden Sun dreams
as we do
and the Moon watches over us all.

Our campfires are small and black.
Only the great Elk is awake to hear the singing.
He turns his antlered head and listens
to the humming, humming, quiet strumming
of the Moon's silver wings.

Spiders nimbly embroider tapestries that will catch morning dew.

Mothers and children snuggle close, safe in each other's arms.

Listen carefully, child.
The singing is everywhere.
The dark trees,
the clouded sky,
the mountains,
the grasslands all echo
the Moon's mellow music
until the last long whisper
that brings the dawn.

JAMAKE HIGHWATER, of Blackfeet/Cherokee heritage, was born in Montana and currently lives in New York City. He is the author of several distinguished books, among them *Anpao: An American Indian Odyssey,* which was named a 1978 Newbery Honor Book.

MARCIA KEEGAN was born in Oklahoma and studied journalism at the University of Mexico. She later studied with Alexey Brodovitch in New York, where she now works as a freelance photographer. Her photographs have appeared in many published works, including *Mother Earth, Father Sky* and *The Taos Indians and Their Sacred Blue Lake.*